ADVANCE PRAISE

"Grace's debut poetry collection ponders language and meaning.

"'I wrote this book because I am interested in how meaning is created,' writes the author in her preface to this new collection. For this emerging poet, meaning is found in the mechanics of human language—specifically word choice and placement—and in the quest to make sense of oneself and the world. The collection is divided into nine sections bearing intriguing, unusual titles, including 'Esemplastic,' 'Limn,' and 'Invariance.' Each section contains a series of poems without titles, numbered in roman numerals. Grace employs a range of poetic forms, from common meter to haiku and pantoums. Some poems contemplate how our relationships with others impact our own identity: 'If you are the center of my map— where / am I?' Others consider the act of writing itself: 'These marks are a compendium of miscellany / a narrative—translucent, pre-existing and replete.' At the close of some sections, the author includes a 'Lyric Glossary' in which she poetically reexamines and reframes specific terms she has used. Grace's poetry is laden with sensuous imagery: 'Ignominious fruit of that garden / my *carmine* lips, your garnet desire.' The most compelling aspect of this ingenious body of verse is the poet's determination to excavate ever deeper layers of meaning; Grace returns to the word carmine in her Lyric Glossary, recalling, 'a rich red to crimson pigment...I bought a dress that made my skin look like cream and my hair look like amber. / I bought it so that your hands on my waist would look like intent—and they did.' The poet moves beyond cold definitions, adding not only personal significance to the term but pinning it to one intimate moment. She poignantly captures how meaning shifts with time: 'a vivid red...I still own that dress. It is packed in a box with other things that don't fit me anymore.' The poet also demonstrates notable technical prowess, as when priming a villanelle to deliver the powerfully philosophical, doubled-barreled refrain: 'What arterial conspiracy was this, aromatic and dusty, rife with pulse and power? / The victor builds the world around himself, calls the edges nothing, the center a flower.' This is the work of an alarming talent.

"An intricate gem of a poetic debut."

—*KIRKUS REVIEWS* (starred review)

"In this sensuous debut poetry collection, *Grenadine and Other Love Affairs*, Carolyn Grace explores meaning through body, image, form, music, myth, and history—and always through language that 'must stretch to convey / only the edge' of the subject ('Grenadine'). In Grace's deft hands, stretch it does—stretch and infuse, suffuse, penetrate, undercut, probe, and play with meaning.

"Grace's love affair with language is most fully reflected in her brilliant deconstruction of definitions and forms. In the Lyric Glossary, she unpacks the multiple—often contradictory— properties of familiar terms (*exposed, inspiration, minute,* for example) as well as opens the richness of unfamiliar terms (*esemplastic, damascene, limn*). Her poetic forms often build on repetitions—pantoums, villanelles, sestinas—that perfectly embody her meaning-making, moving forward and back, inside and out, illuminating complexity. In inhabiting and exploding form, as in her deconstructed sonnets, Grace pursues her larger interests—her unflagging inquiry into who and what she and the world are, were, could be.

"To read these poems is to touch and taste and hold love deeply in body and soul, to celebrate love, unflinching and painful and joyful. 'Poetry,' Grace writes, is 'prayer—a desired exactitude of thought—the magical incantation of the essential ('Delphic', in 'Reverie').' Come, enter this magical, essential world. Let its music sound your depths, its precision sharpen your mind. Then prepare to leave changed, your self challenged and enlarged."

— LIBBY FALK JONES, Professor of English, Emerita, Berea College,
   and author of *Yakety Yak (Don't Talk Back)*

"In *Grenadine and Other Love Affairs* Carolyn Grace invents a form: the lyric glossary. One part definition, one part deconstruction, this new poetic form invites us all to understand the sacred terms of language itself: that every single word holds lifetimes of love and hurt, memory and metamemory, the rarity of connection and the surprise of it. Here is poetry that is finely tuned, from a writer who knows the spiritual urgency of our culture's disconnections, and what we must do to heal them. We must again learn to mean all that we say. What a gorgeous and smart debut."

— REBECCA GAYLE HOWELL, Poetry Editor, *Oxford American* and Assistant Professor of Poetry and Translation, University of Arkansas MFA program

Grenadine
and
Other
Love
Affairs

Grenadine and Other Love Affairs

poems

CAROLYN GRACE

Shadelandhouse
MODERN PRESS

LEXINGTON, KENTUCKY

ISBN: 978-1-945049-35-4
Library of Congress Control Number: 2023931710
Cover art: *Flowers in a Glass Vase, with Pomegranates, on a Marble Balustrade*, 1716,
Rachel Ruysch (1664-1750)
Galleria Palatina/Palazzo Pitti/Florence/Italy, photo credit Scala/Art Resource, NY

Cover and book design: iota books

For my husband, the moon in my sky
&
For my mother, who gave me a prairie

CONTENTS

Bardo

Chiaroscuro

Grenadine

Verisimilitude

Reverie

Limn

Invariance

Preface

I wrote this book because I am interested in how *meaning* is created—meaning like a constellation, like a sonata in D, like the shifting of light, like the faint smell of smoke. And then more—like the heat of the stars, the conductor's baton, the fading to winter, breath caught in the throat. These are all stories which we are telling to each other and to ourselves. We are all making it up as we go along.

What I am trying to say is that we use words (etymology, association, homophones, contextual implication, rhythm) to build structure (sentences, poetic lines, definitions, meter, fragments). We use that structure to build stories. And we use stories to create meaning. None of this is rocket science, really, but little choices change big narratives.

We make choices about syntax that completely alter the sentence, and perhaps the thesis becomes the punch line. We find the same fairy tale in a different culture, and the allusions change even though the language and the happily ever after stay mostly the same. We can switch languages and change the words but keep the meaning. We can keep the words but change the punctuation and lose the plot. Sometimes the structure changes and the words change and the resonance changes and the rhythms change, but the meaning stays the same. That is just good editing (or a hack job). And always, there is something lost, because all words carry different layers of history and emotion and association with them wherever they go.

What I mean is that the stars belong to all of us, but a scientist will tell you stories about light that arrives here from a celestial body that is already dead. A lover might tell stories about a love that is star-crossed or written in the stars, stars in the eyes of the beloved. An academic might tell you about the myths and legends and images that people all over the world have constructed—the meaning they have made of sparks in a changing sky.

And who hasn't made much meaning out of very little? The last straw, the near miss, the chance encounter? Who is not entirely obsessed with their own life story, their reputation, their character, their societal role? What stories do I tell myself about myself? What stories do other people tell about me? And what are the purposes of those stories? Am I absolving myself of guilt? Is someone weaponizing a narrative to gain power or control? Do we both tell the same story about how we fell in love?

When I began writing this book, I decided to unravel certain words both intellectually and emotionally. I wanted to take the structure of formal poetry and push myself to inhabit the form without sacrificing any artistic intent. If it is a sonnet, it has to feel as though nothing was done for the mere sake of meter or rhyme. And if it breaks the rules, there must be meaning in the flaw.

Over time, I found myself deconstructing traditional forms, altering repeated lines more drastically to wring additional meaning from each iteration. This practice developed into a desire to invoke all the dictionary definitions of a given word at once, and if I wanted other people to understand my intent, I needed sources and a glossary. And not just a regular bibliography but a rambling, spiderweb tapestry of source material—part obscure academic mention, part obscure emotional allusion. And not just a regular glossary but a narrative, poetic investigation woven into and around dictionary definitions—a form I call *lyric glossary*.

You might wonder, at this point, what meaning I am actually making or whether this is all purely theoretical. And that would be a reasonable thing to wonder, so I will give you the answer for free: I was working desperately to make sense of myself and the world, to make sense of falling in love and then fighting to keep it, of being a woman and the construction of being a woman and the weight of gendered reality, the fever dream of the early pandemic, the careful examination of my neurodivergent brain, the lived experience of being a writer and artist, the courage I discovered throughout my twenties and the price I paid for needing it. I honestly prefer romantic, but I had to grow into unflinching. It was worth the effort.

I hope that you discover something in this book—something of yourself, someone you love, someone you never understood. I hope that you find a key that fits your lock, flings wide the door you have been afraid to open. And, if nothing else, I hope you find the music of the form, like a heartbeat in the back of your mind.

Grenadine and Other Love Affairs

In the garden there is a woman wearing
sunlight, unselfconsciously reaching out to
taste desire or maybe just touch the surface,
fingertips aching

closer, arm outstretching and eyes alight with
bright awareness. This is the fall of Eden:
not a sordid story of weakness—merely
hunger for beauty.

Esemplastic

I.

I love you like I love
the sea, like I love the sting
of salt on my lips, like I love
its sweep and scope and sand
in my hair. I love you like
I love the ocean, knowing
that I may never live within
a hundred miles of your voice
of the way you crash
into my peripheries again
and again. I can love you
anyway. Because this is loving
like a visitor, like a guest
in a gallery, the chamber
of your heart that sounds
like the ocean when I press
it to my ear. I have lost my fear
of being left out at sea. I know
that we are all just following
the curves of the continents
with the soles of our feet with
our souls in our hands as
the moon tugs our saltwater
toward space. I can love you
this way, knowing that this brine
is both yours and mine knowing
that this water carries us both
knowing that in twenty years,
we will both still look
for the moon.

II.

You hitched a thousand miles
to the soles of your shoes—
unpretentious, worn, used to
muddy. I imagine you are
pleasant and quiet on long trips.

Talk about China. Outline the
architecture of Prague for me,
words tight with the timbre of joy.
We both want Danish childhoods
for the children we don't have.

I've tried to seal it in, this exercise
in loving wisely, loving like a traveler
in a land half remembered from a dream
or a life lived long ago. I've hitched

a thousand miles to this soul; you've left
your fingerprints upon me in the past.
I'm always one to lose track of landscape
in the rush of recognition. Which century?
Which name? Yours or mine?

I work at breathing for a while,
listen to my heartbeat (wonder
if I will ever be near enough
to hear yours and more, to call
it home as I did before in that life
I can't remember now).

I say we should travel together.
You agree. The conversation wanders.

This gift is never named, of course,
but names slip off like clothing.
I remember how to know
in muscle and bone—through
the rhythms we assume
and the mismanaged rhyme
of yours and mine and never
ours to keep. Never mine to lose.
But mine to love, dear traveler.

In spite of detours.
In spite of missteps.
In spite of miles.

III.

We're lost in breath like clouds, a drift of light
on snow, this dust would be mist given heat
or headway.

There are soft shadows at midnight, silhouettes, satin spilled
across your face. I taste the echo of memories that don't
belong to me—trace the line between yours and mine,
follow its sweep and contour.

We traverse your landscape and you take my hand,
let me glimpse your ghosts from the corner of my mind.

I can't show you mine—they are scattered across three states—
but I can tell you about the time I discovered color and knew
I'd be swinging from violet to gold for years to come.

You've spent your life outgrowing buildings on the same street
and I've spent mine memorizing new phone numbers, but now
we're just children at a grown-up time of night,

sharing our secret selves and
testing gravity.

IV.

I stripped naked to write that—didn't expect you to see it—didn't expect to have to explain
the quiet refrain that found the right rhythm (finally) after ages of searching and you were
the subject but it carried the colors of dozens of others and I need you to know

that it's personal to me—not to you—specific but private and pressing but passing and I
cannot be circumspect with my unclothed language lingering in the air
between us. I am better

at candid. And I know you aren't obliged to reply in any way—I am grateful you are gracious,
yet still I am naked and you are quiet and there can be no equality here (like this) when I
have foregone my heart on my sleeve for my soul on my skin. Let me begin again

by saying I never meant you to see those words—wouldn't have chosen to wear my
vulnerability like a badge of honor, wouldn't have risked whatever exists between us but
this is the danger of being a poet: high stakes strip poker—privacy the collateral damage.
I can't quite manage

careless and unembarrassed, but maybe courageous—maybe proud—maybe willing
to take this risk again and again for the rest of my life because at some point you choose
to be safe or stunning and I will always choose running at full speed along
the artistic edge of terrified and truthful.

Forgive me my transparency, but understand—this is how I measure
my success.

V.

I know about water and human
nature, so I knew when you
needed to drift out to sea.

I know about gravity
and mathematics, so I knew
that you'd return with the tide.

I know about fishing
for answers, but I also know
I'll never try to reel you in. Perhaps
just swim alongside for awhile,
allowing space for waves and
differences in wavelength.

Allowing distance to feel safe.

Stars in constellations know
their correlation matters, miles
mean less in larger patterns—time
rather than space, location just
organization of the commonplace.

We lose track of the shoreline,
caught in a quiet current, aware
of our fluid parallel trajectory—

allowing it to speak for itself.

VI.

We're tuned to the same chord, you and I,
moving with the same frequency through
this collection of passing acquaintances.
They don't perceive the counterpoint:

I respond to your rhythm, you shift
toward the sound of my voice—
overtones lingering just beyond
the perception of everyone else—they
think it's the hum of the air conditioning.

I am speaking to someone whose face I have already forgotten when
you catch my eye across the room and there is a sound like an orchestra tuning,
like the roar of numbers when you sing at the strings of an open piano:
octave, fifth, seventh, third—and again but more subtle, more distant and clear.

I hear the chord,
the one to which we both are tuned,
ripple and fill the room.

VII.

Your absence a breeze on the backs
of my knees, and I keep catching
flashes of unmade memories like
an amateur music video on repeat.

I'm in summer dresses and you're in
sunglasses, and I'm in the passenger
seat, watching your profile in peripheral

vision—this whole affair a vivid flash
of color at the edges of my overfull life.

There's this song that reminds me
of the way you talk, of places you spend
your time—reminds me of next summer,

its rush of motion. We live like it's a dying art,
you and I, hands open—eyes wide.

You see, I'd like to be young with you,
strong and careless and broke
and endless in a city of people
on their way to somewhere else. We're

all on our way to somewhere else.

VIII.

I can imagine you there—in a bar with a beer gleaming
amber in the low light, scrawling half-drunk poetry
on a series of napkins and somehow describing
my eyes as I see them, wide and gently tired. You wax

philosophical, vulnerable in this inebriated moment—
yet honest. So honest. And now here's this poem
with your heart and my eyes and I recognize
the precariousness of it all, how I could lose

my balance and fall into your sweetness and
sadness. I know you're steady on your feet
most of the time but I could find you intoxicating
with your kind heart and earnest mind and your
words that remind me so much of myself and

the way that I write—the way that I drift in time
and in poetic lines. Don't pull me too close
to the flame, breath laden with grain I may not
taste, voice laced with amber. It was never

a matter of time or place, we both
ache the same.

IX.

You are soft sleep breathing against
foreign pillows, arms curled around
the space I will someday fill; dreams spill
back and forth—lost in Atlantic tides.

I'm along for the ride. I promise.

And we both know I lose track of myself
every time I see your face, heart naked
in your eyes, in the soft arrangement
of your lips, in the quiet restraint
of your hands that would be buried
in my hair and tracing the line of my back—
were it not for miles and months between us. Still,

I know you so well from here—
in the midst of my private hurricane.

And you see the bend of my spine
in the branching reach of every tree. My
voice in your whisky, my skin a rose garden.

From here, I nearly feel your lips
on my neck, your arms tightening around
my waist as you drift in unconscious currents.
Distance has nothing on heart and will—
the spaces we already fill.

X.

Morning light like mother of pearl
on tile floor, the tidal roar of our
back and forth distant in my ears.

This could take years, if the current
doesn't let us drift. It's a start,
the kind that recalls all the shipwrecks
of our short lives and whispers
they were nothing in comparison.

The kind that rewinds every
extraordinary sunrise and murmurs
they were nothing in comparison.

It begins like the ocean—in the middle.

Honestly speaking, swept off your feet
is something you choose between heartbeats:

heartbeat your voice on the phone
heartbeat my hair in my eyes
heartbeat our feet in the snow
heartbeat we ache for the sky
or maybe its light,
like pearl, like prayer.

It's poetry prior to words,
just rhythm—some impulse
at the base of your heart.

This is the start.
This is the segue.
This could take years.

Palimpsest

I.

Picture pointillism: data conspiring
at one whole image, each entry naught
but sparkle in solitude, a solo voice
aching for choral emphasis.

Steal words like a magpie, eye
collections of fine articulation, exacting
instruments of intent, cleverly
constructed delineators. You

may never need that linguistic
distillation, the quantum solution
to the epistemic problem—
but when you do, you will already

own the word
that fits the lock.

II.

Always a new geometry, a mystery of happenstance—
ink of blood spilled beneath parchment skin.
I catalog these marks (a compendium of miscellany),
each bruise the latent pain from some unconscious impact.

Ink of blood spilled beneath parchment skin:
subdermal sunset, proof of life at varied speeds.
A bruise is latent pain. From those unconscious impacts
trace the horizon of the intellect—constellations of scintilla.

This subdermal sunset is proof of life at varied speeds,
writing and overwriting, endless conjugation of the infinitive.
Trace the horizon. The intellect: constellations of scintilla—
every narrative translucent, pre-existing and replete.

Writing and overwriting is endless conjugation. The infinitive:
to catalog. These marks are a compendium of miscellany,
a narrative—translucent, pre-existing and replete.
Always: a new geometry, a mystery of happenstance.

III.

Constellations borrow their being, ancient
light conceived at distance and given structure
based on culture, language, and season—stories
outlined, transcribed and

spoken. Each voice resonant, overlaying
past inflections, altered in each retelling.
Nothing born in absence of story, we all
borrow our being.

IV.

"To Be" becomes, and
"Has Been" becomes into new
"Is Being." And is.

Bardo

I.

Your grief so fierce it
scalds my heart. To bear witness
is to bear anguish.

II.

Seeking solace in
the Bardo Thödol, you teach
your mind to carry
pain—gentle architecture
to preserve your broken heart.

III.

I sat with you, watched
when you went gray with sadness,
stayed with you, stayed light.

IV.

Your grandparents bought
East-Asian antiques when they
were our age, searching
post-War New York, whispering
Hungarian endearments.

V.

The Japanese vase:
a gift your grandmother will
recognize as love.

VI.

You're in the crisis
between suppressed sorrow and
the first breath of spring—
every nerve exposed, every
truth revealed. Feel this. Move on.

VII.

To be incarnate
is to be always dying,
always being born.

LYRIC GLOSSARY

Bardo (n.)

1. *The intermediate or astral state of the soul after death and before rebirth; Tibetan, literally "between two"*

    a. Me: grasping at theories of liminal space—threshold—transience. Me: having spent the better part of the last decade constructing a practical approach to in-between-ness. Me: still at a loss.

    b. Us: here, lingering barefoot on dirty linoleum, washed out by the yellow overhead light, supported by a laden kitchen counter. Us: practicality slips sideways—crowded into the corner by the breadth of your sorrow.

    c. You: caught between your living grandmother and her eventual death. You: caught between your material life and your structural grief. You: caught between a biological conspiracy of sadness and the reasonableness of your pain.

    d. Me: caught between my conceptual understanding and my practical ignorance. Me: caught between my unconditional adoration of you and the weight of your anguish.

    e. Theory fails me.

Bear (v.)

1. *To accept or allow oneself to be subjected to especially without giving way; to assume or accept; to support the weight of, sustain; to hold above, on top, or aloft; to allow*
    a. The lesson is woven into muscle tissue—which tears in order to grow—which tears in order to withstand—and yet does not yield.
2. *To move while holding up and supporting; to have as a feature or characteristic; to hold in the mind or emotions; to lead or escort; to render or give*
    a. I can be the muscle—I can wrap myself around your ribs, unfurl below your shoulder blades, stabilize your spine, connect to your core—I can pretend that if I am strong enough I can keep your whole self safe and in alignment.
3. *To give birth to; to permit growth of*
    a. Softness can be strength, can be active surrender, can be the sweetness of witness—not structural support, not rigid architecture—but presence and exhale and gift. Every allowance of grace must be directed simultaneously outward and inward.
    b. I can support you from inside my own body.
4. *To be indulgent, patient, or forbearing with*
    a. All of this at once—the gift of liminal space—the theory holds.

Crisis (n.)

1. *The turning point for better or worse in an acute disease or fever; an emotionally significant event or radical change of status in a person's life*
   a. I wake at 2 a.m. roused by an impulse of disquiet. Sliding out of bed I broach the threshold of your room and find you bathed in silvery television light, vulnerable and startled by my unexpected presence. I am also startled and vulnerable.
   b. You pull me into the warmth of your side and unpause Leonard Cohen's somber narration of Tibetan philosophy. Barren landscapes shift across the screen in the color saturation of '90s cinematography.
   c. You watch, as if for any miracle, and I wait, in much the same way, as the moments tilt us quietly toward a different day.
2. *The decisive moment*
   a. And it isn't as if I know where to locate a miracle. But as we wash dishes—open and close the refrigerator door—turn the oven on—set the water to boil—I hold some sliver of prayer in the back of my throat.
   b. I suggest that this is—in fact—all of the grief. Not just the grief of the moment, of death, of loss, but the grief of a life defined by grief—the grief of the little boy, and the lost love, and the whole entire world.
3. *An unstable or crucial time or state of affairs in which a decisive change is impending*
   a. You still—let this thought slide down your spine. I watch your posture shift, just slightly. And then, relief.

Endearment (n.)

1. *A word or an act expressing affection*

    a. You never call me baby but you say my name like it is a prayer, like it is a magic spell, like you could not invent a more beautiful word by which to address me. Like I am the definition of the most beautiful word.

    b. It is hot and humid and very bright outside, the sun reflecting off sidewalk and glass and metal. I eat lunch in a cafe and then wander two doors down to an antique store we visited once together. I recall your grandparents—how they went antiquing in New York City together. I can almost see their house: dark paneling and orange carpet and adornments from all over the world. I think about how you love '70s décor because you love them. I think about how you love bygone eras, and how you love the world.

    c. So I run my fingers over polished furniture and porcelain figurines and gilt picture frames and I try to listen for the whispered intuition: *Buy this for him to give to his grandmother so that she can look at it and think of him. Buy it so that when it is returned to him, he knows that she loved it because he gave it to her.*

    d. I find a little white vase with cheerful green palm trees and cute little houses— World War II era collectible—a pretty piece of historically appropriate sweetness—a name brand she would have known back when it was popular, back when she bought her own antiques, back when her husband was alive and young and held her hand in antique stores.

    e. I buy the vase—the latest act in a lineage of love.

Exposed (adj.)

1. *Open to view*
   a. When the grief breaks open, it does so as laughter. A delighted unraveling. We giggle helplessly, strip off our heavy, let in our lightness. We take internet quizzes at 1 a.m. and we both get strange answers—the unexpected categorization.
2. *Not shielded or protected*
   a. We are caught in an unexpected category all evening.

Incarnate (adj.)

1. *Invested with bodily and especially human nature and form*
   a. I know the theory. I know that to think is to suffer is to be. I know that surrendering desire can reduce the suffering, but I am a human in a body and bodies *desire* things. Minds desire *everything*. Hearts, though...
2. *Made manifest or comprehensible; embodied*
   a. Hearts just love. The theory holds.

Chiaroscuro

I.

I hit the ground at Heathrow, wonder
if I should be wearing makeup, wonder
if you are still my friend (after four years together—
one summer apart). When you meet me

in the crowd you look almost
like yourself, but

on the train into London,
a terse silence descends
and we are already—still—

in angry stalemate. Lilacs
blossom along the tracks.
I imagine their fragrance—
sweetness at the edge
of impervious force.

II.

At Pret-a-Manger I buy cut fruit with pomegranate seeds
and chia coconut pudding and citrus-ginger apple juice—
then we catch a train to Cambridge.

You had been studying there
all summer, and I had been
                              rolling the name around in my mouth
              like hard candy. The landscape stretches—
                    gold undulation…soft sunlight…cerulean ceiling.

I feel the lateness of the season—early autumn in August—
              sooner than my seasonal clock is set to expect.

We walk through streets
made narrow by tall
buildings, storied cliffs
of heavy yellow stone.

        We turn down a narrow
        side street, step through
                a narrow side door.

                Inside—a museum: astrolabes, orrerys, and astrariums—gilded
                mechanics—burnished illuminations of time and distance.
                Some are contrapuntal to the modern map, and some
                a dreamy theme and variation on every modern notion—
                earth-centered music box creations.

                        If you are the center of my map—where
am I?

                        If I am the center of my map—
where do   we
live?

I keep discovering
skewed perspective.

    I keep discovering
    an imaginary edge.

III.

I disintegrate over raspberry
lemonade and pizza.   Sad pop music
plays in the dim, and I   can't
hold my own against it,   anymore.

I tell you   I know:
  a hundred quiet lies—shredding
my trust   by increments.   You tell me
  lying is kinder – than feeling,
                    withstanding
my anger: shredding your will
      by increments.
      I say my anger
has nowhere to go
      in the face of your silence.

You say   silence is the   only   place

you can go

    with me,

anymore.

But – we are in Cambridge.
We are somewhere—together.
And we fight in the cafe
      and in the street,
    and pacing back
    and forth
in the small square
    by the canals.

We think about taking a boat through the city,
                 but we miss our moment.

At least you aren't silent.
At least I'm not stymied.

It's getting late and long shadows
bend around old stone corners.

The flow of words between us slows,
stutters to a halt, as we stumble
over cobblestones.

The small crepe shop is warm
and golden, smells like vanilla
and sugar. We order chocolate
and strawberries. Collapse
at a little outdoor table.

Stare at King's College. It softens—
                 stone lace,
dusky blue-gray silk sliding
under archways. The sunset
makes spilled cream of stoneface.

We soften   lost in place

and all the hundreds of bells in the city
comment together: collective, distinct—
a disagreement of shared intent.

IV.

In Copenhagen, I pretend

      it is our first date. We are so worn
out by each other I am compelled to stand
on my head,
      walk cobblestoned streets
on my hands,
       just to catch your reflexive smile
by the edge, for a breath,
       before it's gone
again.

I ask you what you do for a living.
You shrug awkwardly and try to play

my game. I sparkle like
fool's gold—impersonate charming.

The breeze sharpens and the evening light goes gray.
The dinner reservation never arrives.

Eventually we sit on a bench in a blank
square. We are invisible

to the ebbing crowd. I grow tired
and lonely—quietly sad inside
my makeshift masquerade.

V.

The restaurant is nothing but plants,
warm light, and night-stained planes of glass.

I sit with my back to the wall and watch
with fascination the table just behind you:
graceful Scandinavian models—a Last Supper tableau
in silky, expensive vestment. My dress

is wrinkled—crumpled lace overlay and
a chunky knit sweater. I am not burnished
by the golden light. I am not musical laughter
or languorous gestures or even cheerful
conversation. I am wearing dirty boots. I am
wearing the argument of two hours ago.

You smile at me with tired laugh-lines.
In your sight I am a portrait in a
verdant frame—my Magdalene hair
a filament halo, lavender brush strokes
at the base of my throat, and indigo
shadows behind my eyes.

We submit to a generous repast.
We lose track of our grievances.

Later we spill into our bed
under the eaves and kiss
in the yellow light
of a single lamp.

Grenadine

I.

In the garden there is a woman wearing
sunlight, unselfconsciously reaching out to
taste desire or maybe just touch the surface,
fingertips aching

closer, arm outstretching and eyes alight with
bright awareness. This is the fall of Eden:
not a sordid story of weakness—merely
hunger for beauty.

II.

The murmur of history
        a mendacious mutter,
the clutter of conflict
        meandering latitude.

Ignominious fruit of that garden,
        my carmine lips, your garnet desire,
the grenade that made shards of stained
        glass devotion, compelled the explosion,
the drift in direction—or was it an apple?

This imagery woven
        through parallel stories
and yet so compelling and so overgrown,
        dissonant insinuation of shame not my own:

The apple, the woman,
    the garden, the snake,
the cast of the desert,
    the sanguine affair,
the gleaming of metal,
    the blood in the dust,
the grief and the grief
    and the grief.

When they return seeking relics
        they will find scattered seeds,

your balaustine heart spilling over
        with sweetness, my lips

           in the shape of a prayer.

III.

What arterial conspiracy is this, aromatic and dusty, rife with pulse and power?
Three continents contend with every variety of pilgrim seeking translations of paradise.
The victor builds the world around himself, calls the edges nothing, the center a flower.

But paradise eludes the brave, alludes to wealth, an effusive Babylonian tower.
The philosophical melee circulates, coagulates in holy sites, hemorrhaging divine advice.
What arterial conspiracy is this, aromatic and dusty, rife with pulse and power?

Holy sites with vaulted chambers rush with whispers, clamor on the chosen hour.
Mobs beg for bread, throb with thirst, buy benediction at bitter market price.
The victor builds the world around himself, calls the edges nothing, the center a flower.

The victor defines this heart of conflict, this center of maps—edges exist to be devoured.
Travertine gleams like polished bone, imperial porphyry portentous and precise.
What arterial conspiracy is this, aromatic and dusty, rife with pulse and power?

Byways swell to viscous highways—what artillery was built without the will to overpower?
The pressure builds and breaks at narrow points, the back-and-forth a deadly device.
The victor builds the world around himself, calls the edges nothing, the center a flower.

They still circulate seeking paradise, the word turned meaningless and sour.
Three continents exsanguinated, cultures curated, soil soaked in sacrifice.
What arterial conspiracy was this, aromatic and dusty, rife with pulse and power?
The victor builds the world around himself, calls the edges nothing, the center a flower.

IV.

If you desire absolution, stir
a paste of turmeric and honey,
stain your lips and fingertips gold,
paint your tongue bitter and sweet,
let it fill your throat like a prayer.

What is done is what is done is what is done.

If you desire love, melt
dark chocolate and raspberries,
rose petals, coarse salt, vanilla—
sweet on the tongue, bitter on the breath,
decadence and depth of flavor,
a starburst of caffeine, a floral finish.

What is good is what is good is what is good.

If you desire truth, stand
in your kitchen shadowed by
the overhead light, and cut into
a pomegranate. Observe ruby
chambers—a heart of gems.

Turn each half into a bowl.
Beat the rind with a wooden spoon.

Each seed will spill unbroken—
secrets contained and divulged.
A mouthful is bitter and sweet:
bright rush and dark center.

What is real is what is real is what is real.

V.

He drank from my lips,
traced my blush with his tongue
from the flush of my cheek
to the bud of each breast,
caught a rose in his teeth,
caught my breath in his mouth,
caught my wrist in his fist,
filled my mouth with his pain,
said my name like a prayer,
hid his face in my hair,
let it all come undone.

       Where was I in this?

VI.

I wore the dress that you said made me glow
with rosy and indecent confidence,
the after-dinner drinks and evening snow
an invitation to inconsequence.
It feels like jazz sometimes, you know it does—
it feels like ruby syrup, lazy smoke;
your soft persistent murmuring becomes
the velvet burn of whiskey in my throat
and I give in to heat, of course I do,
with ice out there and laughter on my skin,
intoxicated by the whole of you
and getting caught up contemplating sin.

      We never had a moment quite like this,
       but nothing sparkles more than our near miss.

VII.

Shirley Temple: lackluster virgin cocktail—
what cliché could capture the broken dream of
perfect curls and dimpled compliance better?
Red without flavor,

artificial cherry and bubbles.
This is how you dance to the tune of perfect
woman: keep your ancient and complex flavor
out of the highball.

VIII.

Eve contemplating
shapely crimson mystery
of light on skin. Sweet
challenge and invitation—
a knowledge worth its weight.

So much aliveness,
so much breath in the garden,
the clean scent of earth
the sharp bite of citrus. This
is the heart—just out of reach.

Her whole body knows
there is more to be tasted,
something so lovely
language must stretch to convey
only the edge—

IX.

I thought to myself, this desire is loosely woven,
tensile and light, a silken memory, an arid climate,
a conspiracy of thread. Perhaps the empty spaces
matter more than the points of intersection.

Tensile and light, a silken memory, an arid climate,
the low murmur of history and anguish somehow distant.
Matter: more than the points of intersection.
I stumble through the resonant space between us.

The low murmur of history and anguish somehow distant,
the fabric of our discourse, immediate and warm.
I stumble through the resonant space between us,
allow the shape to change, the drape to shift.

The fabric of our discourse immediate and warm,
a conspiracy of thread. Perhaps the empty spaces
allow the shape to change, the drape to shift,
I thought to myself. This desire is loosely woven.

LYRIC GLOSSARY

Apple (n.)

1. *the fleshy, usually rounded red, yellow, or green edible pome fruit of a usually cultivated tree (genus Malus) of the rose family*

    a. If you decided to meander back through art history, ducking under sweeping sunsets, wriggling through geometric deco designs, tearing your skirt on a dead woman's elaborate broach, you would eventually arrive in a garden. In that garden there is a woman contemplating an apple. Sometimes she is a gleaming pillar of skin and hair, sometimes concealed behind tasteful shrubbery, sometimes adjacent to a beckoning reptile, sometimes adjacent to a blank-faced man. Regardless of the scenery, Eve arrests the eye. We are meant to view her from our external superiority, her naked body, her innocent curiosity, her disobedience. We are meant to desire her and condemn her in the same glance. What happens if we do not?

2. *"The word "apple" once had a broader meaning than it does today. In Old English and in Middle English, the word referred to any kind of fruit..."*

    a. Eve might have been any kind of woman, but history paints all apples and all women with the same brush.

Carmine (n.)

1. *a rich red to crimson pigment made from cochineal*
   a. I bought a dress that made my skin look like cream and my hair look like amber. I bought it so that your hands on my waist would look like intent—and they did.
2. *a vivid red*
   a. I still own that dress. It is packed in a box with other things that don't fit me anymore.

Clutter (n.)

1. *a crowded or confused mass or collection; things that clutter a place*

    a. I brought shame to bed with me last night, let it slide up my skirt, let it twist in my throat, let it catch at my fingers, pull deep in my belly. You brought your fear and it salted your skin, it shrouded your eyes, turned inches of skin into miles of desert. Such a tangle of limbs. Such a tangle of pain. Nothing sweet can grow in such conditions.

Conspiracy (n.)

1. *the act of conspiring together; an agreement among conspirators*

    a. I dreamed I stood on a cement pedestal, raised ten feet off the ground. Everything was gray, a colosseum rising around me in imperious shadow. The night sky was dark with cloud cover, but a grimy light settled on my skin from an unknown source. A group of people approached slowly, carefully—men in dark suits and overcoats, women in low heels and black gloves. They fanned out around the pedestal, gazing up with sharp eyes, murmuring to each other and taking notes in little notebooks. I studied their faces, expecting censure, but I saw admiration. They were writing poems. They were sketching my form. They were calculating my private golden ratio of hip to waist to breast. I looked down and saw that I wore nothing but my own body.

    The conversation grew more heated around me, the faces more irate. They argued about the relative beauty of my shoulders and knees. There was conjecture about the color of my eyes. They said that I was an angel; they said that I was a whore. They said that I must be stupid because I am so lovely. They said that I must be lovely because that is all I am. They said I should be kept in a museum. They said I should be kept in a book. They said I should be kept, somehow, from becoming anything else, anything new or untidy or sacred. They all agreed on that at least. They drew up papers, had them signed and witnessed.

Deft (adj.)

1. *characterized by facility and skill*

    a. I dreamed that a yellow and black snake wound around my bare arm, spoke to me in a mellifluous voice—I turned my eyes away. The voice persisted, gentle and smooth, noble in a way that could break a woman's spirit. I was suffocating with desire; skin crawling with the dry touch of snakeskin—an agony of adoration and disgust. Eventually, at my persistent rejection, the yellow and black head inched closer to my cheek, and whispered in that musical tone "Isn't it strange that I am a snake, but my breath is human breath on your face?"

    I woke with apple juice on my lips and a hole in my heart the size of paradise.

Drape (n.)

1. *arrangement in or of folds*
    a. I bought a dress that made my skin look like silk and my hair look like copper. I bought it so that you would come close enough to smell roses on my throat and whisky on my breath.

2. *a drapery especially for a window*
    a. Moving from chair to window and window to settee, conversation to conversation and back again from settee to chair. Moving from doorway to table, from drink into drink, from conversation to conversation, your regard tangling in the light on my skin, tugging at the shadows between my breasts and beneath my hands and behind my eyes.

3. *the cut or hang of clothing*
    a. I can undress you from across a crowded room. I can change the temperature of your breath. I can trace every well-constructed desire with the corner of my eye. And I could choose to leave the party with the rest of them. Or I could choose to stay until I am the very last guest.

Elude (v.)

1. *to avoid adroitly; evade*
   a. I dreamed that I stood on a pedestal and many eyes were upon me, but they saw only themselves. I bore their scrutiny like a penance for an ancient sin.
2. *to escape the perception, understanding, or grasp of*
   a. I closed my eyes against them. I closed my mind against them. I listened very closely, heard a pulse—my pulse. Swallowed the sound like a panacea, felt it slide down my throat, felt it settle in my belly. Perhaps I was made of marble before. Perhaps I had been plaster or paint. But now—something living.
3. *to defy sense*
   a. I dreamed I wrapped my lips around my own name and gave it life. The people dissolved into points of light. The colosseum unraveled slowly and then all at once. The pedestal nicked my cheek as it fractured into nothing and I tasted pomegranate. At last, all that was left was a vibrant, waiting darkness.

Exsanguinated (n.)

1. *the action or process of draining or losing blood*

    a. The doctor said that I was anemic, and on my way home I stopped at the grocery store and bought a bottle of grenadine. I don't know why. Just corn syrup and red dye and glass, but it caught the light and I liked the color, so I set it on the windowsill in the kitchen. When you came home the next day and told me you had lost your job, I wrapped myself around you and said it would be ok. I juggled bills while you spent weeks on the couch, alternating between depression and rage. I edited your resume, drafted your cover letters, and I bought a bottle of raspberry syrup. I put it next to the grenadine. Sometimes you yelled at me, but I thought it would pass when you got a new job. I forgot to take iron supplements for my anemia, or maybe I chose not to. I bought three bottles of cherry cough syrup and I hid them in the linen closet. You did get a job, finally, but you hated it so much that it made you hate me. I started buying cranberry juice and hiding it in the garage. I could not stop loving you, so I stopped loving myself. I could not stop wanting you, so I stopped wanting myself. Bottles of red liquid in the pantry, under the sink. Bottles of cerise sugar behind the sofa, inside the washer, beneath the guest room bed. I worked harder, stepped lightly, said little, slept less. One afternoon before you got home from work, I was putting away groceries. My hand shook and a bottle of grenadine slipped from my fingers and shattered on the floor. Glass nicked my cheek and blood dripped onto my blouse. I stared at the mess, and as though in a trance I moved through the house. I broke every bottle, I spilled every drop of artificial sweetener and Red 40, let it congeal on the floor, let it pour into air vents, let it stain fabric and paper and the white of the walls. When the whole house dripped crimson, I left. I drove for six days and on the seventh day I rested and I ate a pomegranate straight from the rind, the first I had tasted in years.

Grenade (n.)

1. *a small missile that contains an explosive or a chemical agent and that is thrown by hand or projected*

    a. I kept my bitterness in a small device, carried it in my purse and tucked it into my bedside table. I could not swallow it, I could not close your fingers around it and pull the pin. I could not wrap myself around it only to disintegrate. So sometimes I left it on the kitchen table in the basket of oranges and apples. Sometimes I left it beside the soap in the shower. I felt better knowing that an explosion was possible—that I could effect change if I wanted to. I didn't want to, but I wanted to know that I could. One day I could not bear it any longer, locked in battle with you, caught between the kitchen and the living room, senselessly furious. I held my bitterness in both hands and I pulled the pin. Nothing happened. I tossed it to you and it slipped through your fingers, rolled across the floor. We stared at each other in silence, in expectation. Eventually I knelt on the floor and picked it up, held it in my lap like a baby. I said, "If I had a seed for every time you have broken my heart, I would have a whole pomegranate, broken open."

2. *"our English word 'grenade' comes from the French word for pomegranate"*

    a. You sat down beside me and wrapped your arms around me. You said, "Please forgive me." My bitterness fractured and became a whole pomegranate, broken open, became seeds I could plant in dark soil and from which new life might grow.

Grenadine (n.)

1. *an open-weave fabric of various fibers; grenadine silk*

     a. I found myself on the kitchen floor with my husband's favorite tie in one hand and a pair of shears in the other. I thought perhaps this way I could cut him down to size. The open weave seemed to create a grid of tiny boxes in the fabric—a box for me, a box for the dog, a box for the mistress, a box for the office, a box for muscle cars (maybe several boxes), a box for cutting the lawn, a box for the mortgage and the weather and argyle socks (because he thinks they make him quirky).

2. *a syrup flavored with pomegranates and used in mixed drinks*

     a. I never thought that he was quirky. Not even on our first date when he ordered me a Shirley Temple and a shot of tequila and told me to decide what kind of woman I was. I thought he was bold, but really it was just more boxes I would later shear myself in half to fit inside.

Ignominious (adj.)

1. *deserving or causing public disgrace or shame*
   a. The stage lights are hot and isolating. There are wooden boards underfoot and the sounds of many people moving just beyond the hazy curtain of brightness. I can feel their eyes. I can feel their minds, pressing too closely against my body. I hold out an arm and slowly slide off a glove, silk slipping over my skin for many minutes before it falls from my fingertips. There are gasps from the audience....

Immediate (adj.)

1. *occurring, acting, or accomplished without loss or interval of time; near to or related to the present*

   a. ...I remove a tiny hat with a large feather, a long needle sliding out of the coils of my hair and rolling off the edge of the stage. I unlace an emerald corset, pulling in deep draughts of air as my lungs are able to expand more fully. I tug off a dainty ankle sock, and then a sheer thigh high, then thick woolen tights. As each garment falls to the floor there are murmurs and sighs from the unknowable crowd. Just as I remove one bit of fabric, another appears, capturing my body in variations of clothed.

2. *of or relating to the here and now; existing without intervening space or substance; being near at hand*

   a. I unbutton a linen shirt, tugging at the threads, wrestle a sweater over my head, pull pins out of my hair and feel it cascade down my back, dig my fingers into a too tight braid, watch a bridal veil obstruct my vision with a strange geometry. There is an angry current of sound, voices cracking on censure and command, voices tight with desire.

3. *being next in line or relation*

   a. I yank a skirt down over my hips, toss shoes and rings off the stage, a sparkling ruby, a glass slipper, a combat boot. More and more desperately I struggle, branded T-shirts, blood spattered scrubs, a rain slicker, a designer bra, an immense fur coat, lace and cotton, denim and polyester and leather. The voices grow deafening. I discover that I am afraid.

4. *acting or being without the intervention of another object, cause, or agency; direct; present to the mind independently of other states or factors; involving or derived from a single premise*

   a. I force myself to become still. I feel the rasp of the fabric on my skin as it flickers and changes: a ballgown becomes a leotard, melts into robes, dissolves into a lace negligee, stiffens into a military uniform, disintegrates into a dirty shift. The more still I become, the less I can feel the fabric. The less constrained I am by each layer, each change. I step to the side and slide my fingers around a golden edge, pull myself through an intricate frame and discover that I have stepped through the glass of an elegant mirror. It stands in the middle of the stage, reflecting the audience back to itself.

5. *directly touching or concerning a person or thing*

    a. I turn away from the hazy light and urgent voices, slip past the circumference of the spotlight into softer shadows, purposefully turn my back and dissolve into the wings. I walk into a deep darkness, the polished floorboards becoming polished stone and then moss underfoot.

    A suggestion of cool light expands, and I contemplate a vast garden drenched in moonlight. A soft breeze ripples across my bare skin and carries with it the faint scent of roses.

Mendacious (adj.)

1. *given to or characterized by deception or falsehood or divergence from absolute truth*
   a. We are supposed to desire her and condemn her in the same glance. What happens if we do not?

Verisimilitude

I.

It is my job to contend
with the involuted state—
with the tendency to bend
beneath the psyche's liquid weight.

I'm an involuted state—
pop culture knocking at my door.
Beneath my psyche: liquid wait.
I feel my edges seeking more.

Pop culture knocks at every door
with lists of diatribe, complaint.
I find my edges seeking more:
some holy reason and restraint.

With lists of diatribe (complaint),
with my tendency to bend,
with holey reason, lax restraint—
it is my work to contend.

II.

Take, for example, the opera singer on the stage—
her anguished figure clothed in light and sound,
her voice is her body, but her body is an instrument
for someone else's pain. She is herself and not herself,
she is alone and crowded, she infuses the utterly public
with the bright, sharp edge of the profoundly private.

Her performance feels real because it is real. Privacy
is heartbreak amplified in a second language, the staged
portrayal of an unstageable reality. The glittering public
forget their own breath, wrung by the shocking sound
of an undone woman listening to herself
out loud. She listens because she is the instrument

at the center of a vortex. She is the instrument
of truth dressed in someone else's clothing. Privacy
is just a game that she plays with herself
as she deepens her breath and waits backstage,
as she sharpens her sorrows—when the sound
of her voice is a tightly controlled sob, a public

bloodletting. I used to sing in public,
disguised in borrowed narrative, an instrument
of archetype, tightly wound servant of sound.
I felt every note. Nothing was private
but the heart-stopping fear. I trembled backstage,
afraid of the audience and of myself.

Courage is offering your variable self
up for scrutiny, up for terrifying public
inspection. It is an imperfect art on a moveable stage,

and my body was simply an instrument
strung with intangible effort, nakedly reaching for that private
balance of flow and force, light and dark, breath and sound.

There is a whisper of silence after the final note, then sound—
a clamor of many people recalling the singer to herself.
How she feels in that moment is complex and private,
a masked moment of stillness, a pause for public
comment. She is herself and still an instrument—
a woman in a story simply breathing on the stage.

I am more private now: hopeful and sound,
without wringing on a stage. I am my whole self
beyond that public scene—less instrument, more woman.

III.

You duck intrusive tautologies like your life depends on it.
Your life depends on discerning which propositions are alive.
I am an actress playing the role to which I was born.
You are also playing a role—some days are better than others.

Your life depends on discerning which propositions are alive
in your body. You know which are true because the rest of the time
you are playing a role. Some days are better than others
when your skin is a horizon between more and less genuine.

In your body you know what is true, and the rest of the time
your mind is a diamond—crystalline sharpness, a scatter of light.
But your skin is still the horizon line, more or less genuine
even when you don't want it to be. Even when you don't want it.

My mind is a diamond (crystalline sharpness, a scatter of light)
but I am an actress playing the role to which you were born.
Even when I don't want to be. Even when you don't want to,
you duck intrusive tautologies because your life depends on it.

IV.

Your hip a supple curve

an arc de triomphe in a dress.

Sometimes you're the damsel in distress,

but mostly glowing and prismatic.

We both contain complementary multitudes,

and maybe sometimes I could be your hero.

You have been working to become your own hero

for most of your life, leaning into curves

and writing books to save the multitudes

from each other. And themselves. Undress

your mind and it's prismatic,

a cut-glass rainbow in distress.

It takes an act of god to de-stress

and I make it my mission to play the hero

most days, lost to the prismatic

kaleidoscope of creative curve

appeal. Just unbutton my dress

and kiss me like you mean it, the multitudes

can wait a little longer for the next big thing. There are multitudes

of artists like us after all, swimming in and selling their distress.

Not that I blame them, of course. Somebody suggests that they dress

like sex, become America's sweetheart or hero,

ride public opinion like the parabolic curve

that it is. And if all else fails, break into prismatic

flashes of social-media personality. After all, prismatic

is almost the same as charismatic to the urbane multitudes

of armchair critics with art degrees. Look, I just want to curve

your mouth into delight for a moment. Transform distress
into something vivid and tangible. I don't need to be your hero
or anyone's goddess in glasses and a vintage dress.

Honestly, I'll love you in failure. Undress
your dejected self and take you to bed. Kiss you prismatic
and whisper in your ear that you will always be my hero
just for existing. You are courageous in a multitude
of quiet acts, navigating the maze of everyday distress.
I'll press endearments into your skin, follow every curve.

Don't be the hero with the dressed-
up art. Be the curve in the prism,
love the multitude resulting hues, relinquish your distress.

V.

He is depth and softness, shimmering
sweetness on the tongue, the shadow
of longing and private self-awareness.
She carries the sun on her shoulders.

Sweetness on the tongue and shadows
like an evening gown—he is lunar radiance.
She carries the sun on her shoulders—
an elegant Atlas, an axis personified.

In an evening gown, he is lunar radiance—
a maze of philosophy and fabric,
an elegant atlas, an axis personified.
She glimmers like the reflection of stars.

In a maze of philosophy and fabrication,
of longing and private self-awareness,
they glimmer like a reflection of stars:
depth and softness, shimmering.

Reverie

"To make a prairie it takes a clover
and one bee,—
One clover, and a bee,
And revery.
The revery alone will do
If bees are few."

—EMILY DICKINSON

I.

The endless meadows rise to meet the sky
of eggshell blue, a void of streaming light,
and grasses rasp with insect buzz then sigh
into the breeze that gallops and makes bright
the rippled land. There is no edge to grasp,
there is no point upon which to depend—
just endless blue and blowing seas of grass
beginning at the middle of the end.
Right here, where minute multitudes converge
to orchestrate the hum of summer sound,
the pulsing seconds tremble on the verge
of spacious hours measured underground.

      I am a weightless breath upon the earth
      and every passing inhale, a rebirth.

II.

Jewel tones of old memory,
afternoon gold, a still summer source
where poetry entered, honey in the mouth—
a child's quiet reverie of sweetness.
I am still a tessellation
of linguistic delight.

No surprise of season or delight
but rather ancient, Delphic memory,
given to rippling insight, prone to tessellation.
Bending back and forth as it returns to amber source,
a melting remembered sweetness,
a liquid diction in the mouth.

I carry music in my mouth:
an elegiac meter, a tempo of delight,
the whir of insects, the grassy clover sweetness.
This, the heavy scent of living memory
awash in bronze patina, a source
still tessellating.

The effort is a tessellating
being, a spirit with heart and mouth
and will. She is genius, capricious conduit, not source
but wholly audacious deity of delight,
polishing damascene memory,
sharpening each sweetness.

Bees know sweetness,
know the essential wisdom, know tessellating
geometry, know how to transform ephemera into memory.
How many lives have I lived, honey dripping from my mouth?
How many bridging incantations, the reaching for delight?
How many times pillaged, spilling sweetness
like I'm not the source?

I'm not the source.
Not of lyric sweetness.
Not of longing or delight.
Beauty must always tessellate
finding new mouths
for its memory.

Delight is a perfect shape, the source
of human existence, the memory of original sweetness—
it tessellates indefinitely, lingers in the mouth.

III.

I reach for skies of changing hue—
I've always ached to taste
the butter of the setting sun,
the candied violet trace.

When darkness spills in disarray
above the restless boughs,
I stretch out—in a grassy place—
catch raindrops in my mouth.

And yet—despite my practiced gaze,
my knowledge of the form—
I cannot calm my anxious heart
when facing down—a storm.

IV.

Breath and bark and living soil
    melt to honey—sink
    below surface—swirl through
    archived circumference.

    No self—
        no stiff indifference
        toward all that is animate.

Light coats every plane—transforms into
    sugar—and green—and growing—
    sun becomes shade.

This—the sweetness
    where stillness begins:

LYRIC GLOSSARY

Animate (adj.)

1. *Possessing or characterized by life; alive*
   a. Was I more when I was small—condensed in potent flame of untrained being—small bright sprite of burnished hair and piercing voice and sensorial dismay? Were the afternoons more gold? Were the evenings more silver?

2. *Full of life*
   a. Did the brush and scrape of cloth and dirt and water evoke such a rushing overwhelm that my burden of skin and mind and hunger became too heavy—too frank—too clear and uncompromising? Was this the toil of being very small? Was this the anguish of it?

3. *Referring to a living thing*
   a. Every nerve need not be exposed to thrum with unchecked alertness. It is the work of a moment. It is the work of the moment.

Archived (n.)

1. *A place in which public records or historical materials (such as documents) are preserved; the material preserved*
   a. Moment curves into moment as does everything else in nature—the infant leaf, the robin's neck, the concentricity of elderly trees—and honey—sweetest historical document—preserving the season—the lightest taste of a partial rotation—adjacent to the star upon which we depend.
2. *A repository or collection especially of information*
   a. This—breathing encyclopedia—ancient, chaotic research—collected data of instinct and sediment and breathing bark and aromatic whisper and bone.

Conduit (n.)

1. *A natural or artificial channel through which something is conveyed*
   a. Water decides its means and its ends—bends earth and stone to liquid will—is not dissuaded—is sometimes amenable to diversion—often not.
   b. Electricity possesses neither means nor ends—bends to metal and water and muscle—is not dissuaded—works very hard at mechanical purpose and contrived purpose and human purpose—sometimes leaping great distance for subtle reasons.
2. *A means of transmitting or distributing*
   a. I exist—some fusion of water and electricity—some fusion of means and ends—mechanical purpose and human purpose—straining muscle. Mostly will and diversion—not dissuaded. Sometimes leaping great distance by means of subtle reason—compelled by inner physics.

Damascene (adj.)

1. *Relating to the city of Damascus.*
    a. "Low murmur of history—Anguish muted and distant—I stumble through resonant gaps in the timeline—A clutter of conflict—Meandering platitudes."
    b. "I returned seeking relics to find scattered seeds—A balaustine heart spilling over with sweetness—My lips find the shape of a prayer."
        i. See also *Grenadine*
2. *Used in reference to an important moment of insight, typically one that leads to a dramatic transformation of attitude or belief.*
    a. What voice whispers—an echo in the quiet corridors—between memory and dream? Did He speak to you at midday—an arbitrary highway—an endless whir of minutes? Did She speak your name at midnight—a discreet disclosure of beauty—both invitation and command?
    b. Every life is a creative life. Every choice is a creative choice. Every being is (a) creative being.
    c. Blinding vision, lightning bolt, falling apple—optional.
    d. Inspiration—the quiet intake of breath.
3. *Relating to or denoting a process of inlaying a metal object with gold or silver decoration*
    a. It is the work of a moment. A tilt toward any new version of self. Each backlit blade of grass—etched into resolved relief. The distant appletree—sacred relic. Memory inlaid with summer symbols—the gold afternoon—the silver evening.

Delphic (adj.)

1. *Of or relating to ancient Delphi or its oracle*
   a. I might have been there—cloaked in the fragrant darkness—cloaked in my woman-ness and my reputation and my voice. I might have been there—deep in the earth—riding rising vapor—following the snap of synapse—reaching for obscure patterns—weaving the threads of intellect and inspiration—part poetry—part prayer.

2. *Ambiguous; obscure*
   a. It is, after all, a process of seeking—a parsing of patterns—the leap of faith between detail and structure. Poetry is prayer—a desired exactitude of thought—the magical incantation of the essential.

Diction (n.)

1. *Style of speaking or writing as dependent upon choice of words*
   a. A magical incantation of the essential—the cadential swell of vowel and consonants—sibilance in every language is a hiss and a sigh—breath against lips and teeth—there is a collective inflection of assertion—of revelation—this, a linguistic lineage—every voice—every body—every version of self—holy and resonant—wholly elegant—redefining present and prescient.

2. *The accent, inflection, intonation, and speech-sound quality manifested by an individual speaker, usually judged in terms of prevailing standards of acceptability*
   a. The hiss of the kettle over the flame with the billowing steam and the fragrant leaves and the measured murmur of women.
   b. The hiss of wet wood set to flame as the woman on the pyre transforms into smoke and symbolism.
   c. Later she lives in a different body—buys herbal tea in a cardboard box—has nightmares about fire and betrayal and loss.

Elegiac (adj.)

1. *Written in or consisting of elegiac couplets; noted for having written poetry in such couplets; of or relating to the period in Greece about the seventh century B.C. when poetry written in such couplets flourished*
   a. "For at least 12 centuries, the oracle at Delphi spoke on behalf of the gods, advising rulers, citizens and philosophers on everything from their sex lives to affairs of state. The oracle was always a woman, her divine utterances made in response to a petitioner's request. In a trance, at times in a frenzy, she would answer questions, give orders and make prophecies."
   b. "Some scholars say her divine communications were...interpreted and written down by male priests..."
   c. "In fact, many of the Pythia's answers reported by the literary sources are...elaborate hexameter verses full of metaphors that were not always straightforward but constituted a riddle..."

2. *Of, relating to, or comprising elegy or an elegy; expressing sorrow for something now past*
   a. Even the most powerful woman in one of the most powerful empires in western history is remembered for speaking gibberish that men transformed into prophecy.
   b. Even when she is documented as speaking in her own voice, in her own words, in a rich and ubiquitous meter. Even when her poetry changed the course of war and governance and society.
   c. Women's voices have always existed in the shadow space between immense power and purposeful obliteration.
   d. Do not pretend our rage is modern.

Ephemera (n.)

1. *Something of no lasting significance*
   a. Emily Dickinson at the windowsill or walking through the dawn—writing private poems—filling desk drawers and apron pockets with slips of scribble. Her purpose one of discrete fervor—razor observation—merciless skill—unequivocal elegance.
2. *Paper items that were originally meant to be discarded after use but have since become collectibles*
   a. Her work was unusual for the time—especially the line breaks—especially the use of punctuation—her posthumous publication contentious—her punctuation and queerness edited out of existence—later—carefully—woven back in.

Genius (n.)

1. *An attendant spirit of a person or place*
    a. You will know me by the clover sweetness on your tongue—by the chime of the bell behind your sternum—by the words like smooth stones dropped into your mind while it is clear, and deep, and still. You will know me by the electricity that flickers across your skin—by the shift from puzzling into knowing—by the scrape of the key in the lock of the problem that has held you enthralled all this time.
    b. I already know you.
2. *A peculiar, distinctive, or identifying character or spirit; the associations and traditions of a place; a personification or embodiment especially of a quality or condition*
    a. I would rather have a genius than be one.
    b. A genius like a little white cat—she sits on my lap only when she wishes—purring like a natural constant—soft and warm and belonging to herself.
    c. A genius like a mermaid of living gemstone—swirling amber hair—jade eyes—garnet lips—a lapis lazuli tail—she sings songs that I cannot hear but which get into my saltwater blood—get into my saltwater tears—flood me like a grotto at high tide.
    d. A genius like a honeybee—cheerfully meandering past each lovely being in the meadow—tasting and visiting and lingering briefly—returning home with some essential souvenir.
3. *A single strongly marked capacity or aptitude; extraordinary intellectual power especially as manifested in creative activity; a person endowed with extraordinary mental superiority*
    a. Condensed in potent flame of untrained being—there was an aptitude for beauty—an aptitude for poetry—the first notebook I ever owned contained an Emily Dickinson poem—written in my mother's hand.
    b. Just like in the fairy tales—magic has a price. The little body containing the big beauty is still little—is still soft and strange and animal. For every gold afternoon—a feverish heatstroke daze. For every silver evening—a listless enervating fatigue.

Minute (adj.)

1. *Very small; infinitesimal*
   a. The little body containing the big beauty is still little—endless is macro and endless is micro—infinite is external and infinite is internal—who can blame the child for unease in human form? She has not been here very long—is not yet used to boundaries around her infinity.
2. *Of small importance; trifling*
   a. Did the brush and scrape of cloth and dirt and water evoke such a rushing overwhelm that my burden of skin and mind and hunger became too heavy—too frank—too clear and uncompromising? Was this the toil of being very small? Was this the anguish of it?
      i. See also "Animate"
3. *Marked by close attention to details*
   a. I still navigate sensorial menagerie—the loud and the sharp and the harsh—the swish and the brush and the slam—the satin and the sweet—the sweep and the rush—the bitter and bulky and bright.
   b. Language helps me do this.

Orchestrate (v.)

1. *To compose or arrange (music) for an orchestra; to provide with orchestration*
   a. If color is frequency and frequency is also vibration and vibration is also sound then every color has a voice—lost in translation between electromagnetic and mechanical waves.
2. *To arrange or combine so as to achieve a desired or maximum effect*
   a. How frequently—despite my efforts—am I lost in translation?

Patina (n.)

1. *A usually green film formed naturally on copper and bronze by long exposure and often valued aesthetically for its color; a surface appearance of something grown beautiful especially with age or use*
   a. Breathing encyclopedia—sun-drenched and burnished—light transformed into molten being—cast in shining summer bronze—grown green and beautiful with age and use.
2. *An appearance or aura that is derived from association, habit, or established character*
   a. Living memory—collective and concrete—patterned and textured—curated and recreated—in every leaf and bloom.

Reverie (n.)

1. *A state of dreamy meditation or fanciful musing*

    a. "To make a prairie it takes a clover and one bee,—

2. *A daydream.*

    a. One clover, and a bee,

    And revery.

3. *A fantastic, visionary, or impractical idea*

    a. The revery alone will do

    If bees are few."

    XCVII —Emily Dickinson

Spacious (adj.)

1. *Vast or ample in extent*
   a. The wind in the grass, a mechanical wave—symphonic rush—roving past the edge of visual perception—sweeping away on some unknown errand.
2. *Large or magnificent in scale; expansive*
   a. The biggest beauty is infinitely big.
   b. The biggest beauty is infinitely small.

Tessellation (n.)

1. *Mosaic; a surface decoration made by inlaying small pieces of variously colored material to form pictures or patterns; a covering of an infinite geometric plane without gaps or overlaps by congruent plane figures of one type or a few types*

    a. "When I was small—condensed in potent flame—sprite of burnished hair and piercing voice and sensorial dismay—the afternoons more gold—the evenings more silver—it was an aptitude for beauty—an aptitude for poetry—the first poem I ever knew—a revery—written in my mother's hand."

    b. "Each moment curves into honey—the lightest taste of a partial rotation—this—ancient research—sun-drenched and burnished—grown green and beautiful with age and use."

    c. "I might have been there—cloaked in my woman-ness and my reputation and my voice—sometimes leaping great distance by means of subtle reason—transformed into smoke and symbolism—speaking gibberish for the world to translate—a magical incantation of the essential—redefining present and prescient."

    d. "I exist—some fusion of water and electricity—the leap of faith between detail and structure—a tilt toward any new version of self—I taste its clover sweetness on my tongue."

Limn

I.

I'm still caught squarely in the hazy gold of August,
tracing shady peripheral pathways, avoiding mud and
watching the swirling scissor blades of grass. There is
a lot to worry about. I listen to the grasshopper's buzz.

Tracing shady, peripheral pathways, avoiding mud and
mosquito bites, there is always an itch in mind, always
a lot to worry about, and I listen to the grasshoppers buzz
louder than headlines. All the light sharpens all the shadows.

Mosquito bites (there is always an itch in mind) always
an interrupting discomfort, but the path plays out, quiet
louder than headlines. All the light sharpens all the shadows:
bluegrass state read with their generation's breath-less dead.

Interrupting discomfort, the path plays out quietly.
I watch the swirling scissor blades of grass in this
bluegrass state, red with my generation's breathless dead.
I still, caught squarely, in the hazy gold of August.

II.

We know how to bring the quiet inside with us, these days.
Everything is better than it was last summer—
you make me laugh and we watch vintage television together.
Last summer we fought across two continents and seven countries.

Everything is better than it was last summer,
except for the plague, and the Nazis, and the burning of Rome.
Last summer, we fought across two continents and seven countries.
This summer, we stop to breathe; unpack in our apartment.

In spite of the plague and the Nazis and the burning of Rome,
we go on walks. We let our little dog bounce through tall grass
this summer. We stop to breathe, unpack our apartment,
brush burrs out of the dog's coat, and fall asleep together.

We go on walks and let our little dog bounce. Through tall grass
I hear your laughter. Later we'll watch vintage television,
brush burrs out of the dog's coat, and fall asleep together.
We know how to bring the quiet inside with us, these days.

III.

These days are pinpricks of light at the bottom of a bucket
and time pours through like water.
Despite the strange mechanics at work out there,
we wash the dishes, write papers, and ask each other what to have for dinner.

And time pours through like water
as weeks stretch into months stretch into the hazy horizon line.
We wash the dishes, write papers, and ask each other what to have for dinner
because that is what we know to do. That is how we live.

As weeks stretch into months stretch into the hazy horizon line,
I have befriended my anxiety—given it space at the table
because that is what I know to do. That is how I live
in the midst of an intangible crisis—I make space.

I have befriended my anxiety and given it space at the table
despite the strange mechanics at work out there.
In the midst of an intangible crisis I make space
these days—for pinpricks of light at the bottom of a bucket.

IV.

Here at the glowing threshold of autumn—
the field washed in gold for a decade of breaths.
Daylight shrinks imperceptibly, then all at once
by those ancient mechanics, gold silvers to frost.

The field washed in gold for a decade of breaths
(I still clutch my coat when the shadows gain ground).
By those ancient mechanics gold silvers to frost,
and the tree by the street turns a purposeful red.

I still. Clutch my coat. When the shadows gain ground
the whisper of ice is a sharp-edged demand.
The tree by the street turns a purposeful red
and I think that bright living holds dying in view.

The whisper of ice is a sharp-edged demand—
daylight shrinks imperceptibly, then all at once.
I think that bright living holds dying in view,
here, at the glowing threshold of autumn.

V.

Silvered wisps of cloud swirl across the November moon.
Never mind the poisoned breath, the darkness that I've learned to fear—
I am limned by the romance of alone and unmoored.
There is no story without a shadow to cast or to claim.

Never mind the poisoned breath, the darkness that I learned to fear
when I grew up. When I was young I understood:
there is no story without a shadow to cast or to claim.
Now I am twice as strong, but half as brave at night.

I grew up. When I was young I understood
enchantment is a shade of light—bright as water, clear as glass.
Now I am twice as strong but half as brave. These nights
spin out fragile and singing, a bolt of indigo silk, a glitter of stars.

Enchantment is a shade of light as bright as water, clear as glass.
I am limned by this romance of alone and unmoored:
spun out fragile and singing, a thread of indigo silk, a glitter of stars,
a silvered wisp of cloud swirled across the November moon.

Invariance

I.

I'm aching for you even when I shift
away from touch and cannot meet your eyes—
call this an anguished game we both despise.
You reach for me—I freeze—and then we drift
into a glossy nothing—edgeless rift.
There is no bridge or boat we can devise,
no careful plan or map to analyze
that brings us back to us—embrace, desist.

I'm sitting with my back against the wall.
You're walking toward the door to get your shoes.
With you, I'm much too much and also small—
I default to the crimes that I excuse.
You fiercely blame yourself and I recall
that when I play to win, I always lose.

II.

You're still avoiding tangles, heavy words:
my razor mind, your gaze like satin smoke,
adumbral eyes and hands like hummingbirds—
perhaps I am the chain around your throat.

We're smothered by a pattern with no name,
and yet we drift—like winged things—toward light.
We've lost ourselves in restless, helpless blame;
paralysis is quantum fight and flight

condensed into a liminal debate.
Our symmetry is harshly misapplied,
our chemistry a caustic, labile state—
the paradox of worthlessness and pride.

You wrap me in your arms and hold me still.
I acquiesce to space you cannot fill.

III.

I watch him as he turns his head away,
the long line of his neck a curve of light,
expressions flicker and deep shadows play
across his face. Perhaps I am the night—
the blaze of stars, the snow in glowing drifts,
the air like glass—and he's the wayward moon,
part fluid lord who sets my heart adrift,
part anchor in the dark (a lunar swoon).
I know there's more to us than what exists
within the storied physics we construct—
this gravity pulls everything, persists;
it's bigger than the sky, as vast as trust.

      You hold my gaze with eyes as deep as space,
      time stills—a singularity of grace.

IV.

I reach for you with hands that hold
what isn't there—your phantom curves
a silhouette in which you glow—
your eyes are soft, your throat exposed.
We make believe. We make belief
of murmured need and hungry reach.
I trace your waist, the sketch a blur
of tangled truths—you gasp against
my view of you, the love that holds
you near yourself. The effort was
a battlefield, but now, just sky—
a light swept sea. And here we are.

      You come to me like breaking dawn.
      You know—I've loved you—all along.

Acknowledgments

Writing any book is an undertaking, but writing my first book was truly a gauntlet, and being me, I decided to write it close to the edge of both my intellectual capacity and what my heart could bear. Any person walking such a path needs all kinds of support, and I was lucky to have so many people who both challenged and encouraged me along the way.

First, I have to thank Virginia Underwood. You picked me out of a crowd and you have stayed with me all these years, believing in me and my writing and the book that wouldn't exist if you hadn't asked me to write one. Thank you for consistently trusting my artistry and for encouraging me to trust my creative vision.

Second, thank you to Libby Jones. I can't begin to describe the breadth of your impact on my life, but I would not be this writer without your years of friendship, support, and careful, respectful insight.

Thank you to the Kentucky State Poetry Society (KSPS) for awarding me first place in the 2015 President's Prize Contest for an earlier version of "Esemplastic I" when it was still called "Like the Sea." It was subsequently published in *Pegasus*, the KSPS poetry journal, Vol. 44 No. 3. Further, I owe a tremendous debt of gratitude for the KSPS conference in 2018, where I first met both my future publisher and my future graduate school. Being a featured reader that fall had a truly significant impact on my career as a writer.

Thank you to the Bluegrass Writers Studio at Eastern Kentucky University and especially to Young Smith, Julie Hensley, Carter Sickels, and R. Dean Johnson. You challenged and encouraged me, and I am so grateful for the unique lessons I learned from each of you.

Thank you to Women Writing for (a) Change for their kindness and enthusiasm.

Thank you to Loretta for introducing me to my brain.

Thank you to Rebecca Gayle Howell for the perfect lecture at the perfect time.

Thank you to Will for explaining theoretical physics over and over again and for always being available when I need to translate science into metaphor and back again.

Thank you to Steven for being a part of our family, bringing your wonderful energy into our bubble, and loving my mother so much.

Thank you to my mother, Ayla Rose, for pretty much everything. Thank you for nurturing my love of reading and writing. Thank you for reminding me of who I am every time I start to forget. Thank you for walking this road with me. Words will always be inadequate when it comes to thanking you.

And thank you to Grant. You are my friend, teacher, partner, and now my husband. Thank you for your unwavering, fierce belief in my talent and intelligence. Thank you for sincerely desiring my happiness and peace. Thank you for your courage and strength as we have grown up together. I love you with all my heart.

Author's Note on the Cover Art

Flowers in a Glass Vase, with Pomegranates, on a Marble Balustrade, by Rachel Ruysch, painted in 1716, has a concretely descriptive name, but the painting itself is layered and complex. At a basic level, it is technically stunning—each flower and insect rendered true to life. It is this technical mastery that draws the eye through the structure of the arrangement as a whole, a structure that surpasses the bounds of any traditional floral arrangement of that time, defying gravity and season.

If her art defies gravity, Ruysch herself defied inertia. She began painting in 1679, when she was 15, and continued to work until she was 83. She married later in life (especially for her time) and had 10 children, but her wildly successful career allowed her to pay for childcare so she could continue painting. Ruysch's technical precision began with the scientific examination of specimens collected by her botanist father, but her whimsical use of color and structure is entirely her own. Reading about her life feels like a benediction, a portrait of a woman overcoming false dichotomies. And that same intensity is reflected in her art—effusive and delicate, the light both brilliant and focused, the shadows deep and suggestive of details just beyond our perception.

In the context of this book, those elements of the way Ruysch lived her life—and many details in the painting itself—suggest the nature of this written work. At a basic level, I have striven to craft each poem with as much technical perfection as I am capable of, and in that context, deviations from formal structure can be examined with the knowledge that the writer (artist) is intending that deviation as meaningful. A woman who can paint a perfect rose can be trusted to know that her arrangement defies gravity—heavy blooms held aloft by no apparent means. A woman who can write a classical sonnet with modern language can be relied upon to remember the number of syllables in a haiku. Beyond the structural intricacies at the macro and micro levels, this painting converses easily and naturally with all the title words that I have used in this book. I invite you to join that conversation.

Sources

Dictionaries:

    https://www.merriam-webster.com/

    https://www.dictionary.com/

    https://www.etymonline.com/

Esemplastic:

    The Evolution of the Term "Esemplastic"
    https://www.jstor.org/stable/3715968

    The Anableps Guide to Serendipity: Intentional Serendipity as Creative Encounter—
    A Decolonised, Literary Perspective from The Art of Serendipity
    https://link.springer.com/book/10.1007/978-3-030-84478-3

    Mid-Atlantic Ridge
    https://www.britannica.com/place/Mid-Atlantic-Ridge

    Counterpoint
    https://www.britannica.com/art/counterpoint-music

    Anna Sun
    https://www.youtube.com/watch?v=qDVW81bXoos

    Queen Mary's Garden
    https://www.royalparks.org.uk/parks/the-regents-park/things-to-see-and-do/gardens-
    and-landscapes/queen-marys-gardens

Palimpsest:

    A Sunday on La Grande Jatte — 1884
    https://www.artic.edu/artworks/27992/a-sunday-on-la-grande-jatte-1884

Epistemology
https://plato.stanford.edu/entries/epistemology/

If You Don't Understand Quantum Physics, Try This!
https://www.youtube.com/watch?v=Usu9xZfabPM

What is quantum computing?
https://www.ibm.com/topics/quantum-computing

Bardo:

The Tibetan Book of the Dead (1994) - Part 1 of 2
https://www.youtube.com/watch?v=f8jn4Yp4Kj8

The Tibetan Book of the Dead (1994) - Part 2 of 2
https://www.youtube.com/watch?v=DuQMU6O8c2s

Bardo Thodol
https://www.britannica.com/topic/Bardo-Thodol

Liminal Space: What Is It And How Does It Affect Your Mental Health?
https://www.forbes.com/health/mind/what-is-liminal-space/

Chiaroscuro:

How Chiaroscuro Emerged From the Dark to Become One of the Most Iconic Painting Styles
https://mymodernmet.com/chiaroscuro-painting-technique/

What exactly is bel canto? It's a way of singing and, for some, an addiction.
https://www.washingtonpost.com/lifestyle/style/what-exactly-is-bel-canto-its-a-way-of-singing-and-for-some-an-addiction/2019/03/28/9a97e9d0-5055-11e9-a3f7-78b7525a8d5f_story.html

Color and Chiaroscuro in the Professional Singing Voice
https://singalexander.wordpress.com/2016/09/25/color-and-chiaroscuro-in-the-professional-singing-voice/

Whipple Museum of the History of Science
https://www.whipplemuseum.cam.ac.uk/

The Poem as Liminal Place-moment: John Kinsella, Eavan Boland, Christopher Dewdney, and Mei-mei Berssenbrugge
https://www.academia.edu/4048255/The_Poem_as_Liminal_Place_moment_John_Kinsella_Eavan_Boland_Christopher_Dewdney_and_Mei_mei_Berssenbrugge.

Grenadine:

A Web of Word Connections: "Apple"
https://medium.com/the-philipendium/a-web-of-word-connections-apple-94f9e95ec0b6

Where the word 'apple' came from and why the forbidden fruit was unlucky to be linked with the fall of man
https://www.scmp.com/magazines/post-magazine/article/3139890/where-word-apple-came-and-why-forbidden-fruit-was-unlucky

The Fall of Man (Rubens)
https://en.wikipedia.org/wiki/The_Fall_of_Man_(Rubens)#/media/File:Peter_Paul_Rubens_004.jpg

Pomegranate Etymology
https://www.etymonline.com/word/pomegranate?ref=etymonline_crossreference

Why a pomegranate?
https://www.ncbi.nlm.nih.gov/pmc/articles/PMC1118911/

Intro to Pomegranate
https://www.alcademics.com/2012/12/intro-to-pomegranate.html

The History of Grenadine Use in Cocktails: Theories and Conclusions
https://www.alcademics.com/2012/12/the-history-of-grenadine-use-in-cocktails-theories-and-conclusions.html

When Did Grenadine Become an Artificial Ingredient?
https://www.alcademics.com/2012/12/when-did-grenadine-become-an-artificial-ingredient.html

How to Remove Pomegranate Seeds and Make Grenadine the Easy Way
https://www.alcademics.com/2012/12/how-to-remove-pomegranate-seeds-and-make-grenadine.html

The History of Grenadine Use in Cocktails: Literature Review
https://www.alcademics.com/2012/12/the-history-of-grenadine-use-in-cocktails.html

Aphrodite
https://www.britannica.com/topic/Aphrodite-Greek-mythology

The Pomegranate: A New Look at the Fruit of Paradise
https://journals.ashs.org/hortsci/view/journals/hortsci/42/5/article-p1088.xml

From The Bronze Age To The American Table: A History Of The Pomegranate
https://www.tastingtable.com/984460/from-the-bronze-age-to-the-american-table-a-history-of-the-pomegranate/

Pomegranates: Rich In History and Taste
https://www.nytimes.com/1979/10/31/archives/pomegranates-rich-in-history-and-taste.html#:~:text=THE%20pomegranate%2C%20one%20of%20the,apple%2C%E2%80%9D%20the%20alternate%20appellation.

Grenadine Fabric: History, Tradition, and Ties
http://journal.styleforum.net/grenadine-fabric-history-tradition-and-ties/

How a Word For "Blood" Came to Mean "Optimistic": The Odd History of "Sanguine"
https://www.merriam-webster.com/words-at-play/sanguine-word-history

Travertine and Fifteenth-Century Roman Architecture from Reviving Antiquity with Granite:
Spolia and the Development of Roman Renaissance Architecture
https://doi.org/10.1017/arh.2016.5

Imperial purple porphyry: the archaeology of the emperors' building stone (Society of Antiquaries of Newcastle upon Tyne Lecture)
https://www.ncl.ac.uk/events/public-lectures/archive/item/2011imperialpurpleporphyry
thearchaeologyoftheemperorsbuildingstone.html

Her Body and Other Parties
https://carmenmariamachado.com/her-body-and-other-parties

Abandon Me
https://www.melissafebos.com/abandon-me

Where Poetry Begins: Eavan Boland in Conversation
https://poets.org/text/where-poetry-begins-eavan-boland-conversation

Eden
https://www.youtube.com/watch?v=LApkj1GiEzA

Verisimilitude:

Truthlikeness
https://plato.stanford.edu/entries/truthlikeness/

Verisimilitude
https://www.britannica.com/art/verisimilitude

PHILOSOPHY - Ludwig Wittgenstein
https://www.youtube.com/watch?v=pQ33gAyhg2c

Mechanisms of social change
https://www.britannica.com/topic/social-change/Mechanisms-of-social-change

Andrew Sofer - Dark Matter: Invisibility in Drama, Theater, and Performance
https://www.youtube.com/watch?v=pPmVdqjG2XE

Stray City
http://www.chelseyjohnson.com/stray-city

Autism, Masking, & Trans Identity
https://medium.com/age-of-awareness/autism-masking-trans-identity-5cc1987ca69b

What is Masking and Why Do Neurodivergent People Do It?
https://www.lgbtqandall.com/what-is-masking-and-why-do-neurodivergent-people-do-it/

Performative Acts and Gender Constitution: An Essay in Phenomenology and Feminist Theory
https://www.jstor.org/stable/3207893

Atlas
https://www.worldhistory.org/Atlas/

Atlas and Axis
https://www.jstor.org/stable/638657

Reverie:

"To make a prairie it takes a clover and one bee" J 1755/F 1779
The Poems of Emily Dickinson, edited by Thomas H. Johnson, Cambridge, Mass.: The Belknap Press of Harvard University Press, Copyright © 1951, 1955, 1979, 1983 by the President and Fellows of Harvard College.

Chapter 3 Greek Sources from Ancient Prophecy: Near Eastern, Biblical, and Greek Perspectives
https://doi.org/10.1093/oso/9780198808558.003.0003

For Delphic Oracle, Fumes and Visions
https://www.nytimes.com/2002/03/19/science/for-delphic-oracle-fumes-and-visions.html#:~:text=For%20at%20least%2012%20centuries,response%20to%20a%20petitioner's%20request.

Elegy
https://www.britannica.com/art/elegy

Hexagon
https://www.britannica.com/science/hexagon

Breakthrough Study Reveals Biological Basis for Sensory Processing Disorders in Kids
https://www.ucsf.edu/news/2013/07/107316/breakthrough-study-reveals-biological-basis-sensory-processing-disorders-kids

Take a Tour of Tessellations, the Mathematical Art of Repeating Patterns
https://mymodernmet.com/tessellation-art/

The lost girls: 'Chaotic and curious, women with ADHD all have missed red flags that haunt us'
https://www.theguardian.com/society/2020/nov/02/the-lost-girls-chaotic-and-curious-women-with-adhd-all-have-missed-red-flags-that-haunt-us

The Occuplaytional Therapist
https://www.facebook.com/occuplaytional

Big Magic
https://www.elizabethgilbert.com/books/big-magic/

Your elusive creative genius
https://www.ted.com/talks/elizabeth_gilbert_your_elusive_creative_genius

The Posthumous Discovery of Dickinson's Poems
https://www.emilydickinsonmuseum.org/emily-dickinson/poetry/the-poet-at-work/the-posthumous-discovery-of-dickinsons-poems/

A Guide to Emily Dickinson's Collected Poems
https://poets.org/text/guide-emily-dickinsons-collected-poems

Emily Dickinson's Herbarium: A Forgotten Treasure at the Intersection of Science and Poetry
https://www.themarginalian.org/2017/05/23/emily-dickinson-herbarium/

Emily Dickinson Isn't Difficult—She's Just Misunderstood
https://electricliterature.com/wild-nights-with-emily/

Renascence
https://www.poetryfoundation.org/poems/55993/renascence

Limn:

Wittgenstein in Norway
https://bcm.bc.edu/issues/fall_2004/ll_wittgenstein.html

Time-Lapse Spread of COVID-19 By County (Cumulative)
https://publichealthmaps.org/motw-2021/2021/10/13/13-october-time-lapse-spread-of-covid-19-by-county-cumulative

epiphany
https://www.youtube.com/watch?v=DUnDkI7l9LQ

Indoor Air and Coronavirus (COVID-19)
https://www.epa.gov/coronavirus/indoor-air-and-coronavirus-covid-19

Invariance:

The Secure Relationship
https://www.instagram.com/thesecurerelationship/

The female burden of neurodiversity: Society is failing women with neurodevelopmental disorders
https://theweek.com/articles/878719/female-burden-neurodiversity

A Quantum Physics Approach to a Singularity Problem
https://scitechdaily.com/a-quantum-physics-approach-to-a-singularity-problem

Noether's Theorem: How Symmetry Shapes Physics
https://www.cantorsparadise.com/noethers-theorem-how-symmetry-shapes-physics-53c416c1f19c

APA Dictionary of Psychology: Invariance
https://dictionary.apa.org/invariance

APA Dictionary of Psychology: Transformation
https://dictionary.apa.org/transformation

24 - Conceptual Metaphor from Part IV - Conceptual Mappings from The Cambridge Handbook of Cognitive Linguistics
https://doi.org/10.1017/9781316339732.025 pp. 385 - 406

Sources for Note on Cover Art

Old Masters: Overlooked Women Artists
http://www.gadflyonline.com/home/01-14-02/ftr-women.html

For the First Time in Its 200-Year History, the Rijksmuseum Features Women Artists in 'Gallery of Honour'
https://www.smithsonianmag.com/smart-news/rijksmuseum-will-display-work-women-artists-its-gallery-honour-first-time-180977209/

For the First Time Ever, the Rijksmuseum Will Hang Works by Female Dutch Masters in Its Most Prestigious Gallery
https://news.artnet.com/art-world/rijksmuseum-female-artists-gallery-of-honor-1950686?

Rachel Ruysch, Fruit and Insects
https://www.youtube.com/watch?v=EK-h6cZCXrs

Know the Artist: Rachel Ruysch
https://www.youtube.com/watch?v=UHBB483Dcdw

Rachel Ruysch: Painter of the court and mother of 10 | National Gallery
https://www.youtube.com/watch?v=GqToJVkIxU4

Poetic Forms

Common Meter
Deconstructed Sonnet
Haiku
Italian Sonnet
Lyric
Lyric Glossary
Pantoum
Recipe
Sapphic Form
Sestina
Sonnet
Tanka
Villanelle

About the Author

Carolyn Grace began writing poetry as a child, and has been completely in love with language ever since. Grace graduated from Berea College with an undergraduate degree in English composition and a minor in music performance. She went on to complete her master of fine arts in creative writing through the Bluegrass Writers Studio at Eastern Kentucky University. Grace lives in Northern Virginia with her husband, Grant, and their dog, Fitzwilliam, who appears to be aware that he is named after literary royalty and acts accordingly. This is her debut book of poetry.

CPSIA information can be obtained
at www.ICGtesting.com
Printed in the USA
JSHW082104170723
44868JS00003B/261